GREAT MINDS® WIT & WISDOM

Grade 1 Module 4
Cinderella Stories

Student Edition

GREAT MINDS

Great Minds® is the creator of *Eureka Math*®,
Wit & Wisdom®, *Alexandria Plan*™, and *PhD Science*®.

Published by Great Minds PBC
greatminds.org

© 2023 Great Minds PBC. All rights reserved. No part of this work may be reproduced or used in any form or by any means—graphic, electronic, or mechanical, including photocopying or information storage and retrieval systems—without written permission from the copyright holder.

Printed in the USA

A-Print

1 2 3 4 5 6 7 8 9 10 QDG 27 26 25 24 23

979-8-88588-721-2

Student Edition

Handout 2A: Fluency Homework

Handout 3A: Story Map

Handout 6A: Opinion Sandwich Chart

Handout 7A: Objects for Retelling

Handout 7B: Cendrillon Opinion Paragraph

Handout 8A: Focusing Question Task 1 Evidence Organizer

Handout 9A: Cinderella and Cendrillon Experience Cards

Handout 9B: Opinion Writing Checklist

Handout 10A: Objects for Retelling

Handout 11A: Fluency Homework

Handout 11B: Commas in a Series

Handout 13A: Story Map

Handout 13B: The Beary Godfather

Handout 14A: Word Cards

Handout 15A: Focusing Question Task 2 Evidence Organizer

Handout 16A: Cinderella and Ella Experience Cards

Handout 16B: Opinion Writing Checklist

Handout 17A: Fluency Homework

Handout 17B: Word Cards

Handout 18A: Story Map

Handout 18B: Pronoun Practice

Handout 19A: Adelita Action Cards

Handout 19B: Pronoun Practice

Handout 21A: Venn Diagram

Handout 21B: Ella and Adelita Experience Cards

Handout 21C: The Rebozo

Handout 22A: Fluency Homework

Handout 23A: Story Map

Handout 24A: Pear Blossom Action Cards

Handout 24B: Focusing Question Task 3 Evidence Organizer

Handout 25A: Illustration Scavenger Hunt

Handout 25B: Content Word Sort

Handout 26A: Opinion Writing Checklist

Handout 26B: Sentence Frames

Handout 27A: "900 Cinderellas"

Handout 28A: Word Cards

Handout 30A: Textile Patterns

Handout 30B: End-of-Module Task Evidence Organizer Chart

Handout 32A: Opinion Writing Checklist

Handout 34A: Socratic Seminar Self-Reflection

Volume of Reading Reflection Questions

Wit & Wisdom Family Tip Sheet

Name: _____

Handout 3A: Story Map

Directions: Draw a picture or write to show the elements of the story.

Cinderella Story Map

Name:

Handout 6A: Opinion Sandwich Chart

Directions: Use the Opinion Sandwich Chart to help retell and write an opinion paragraph.

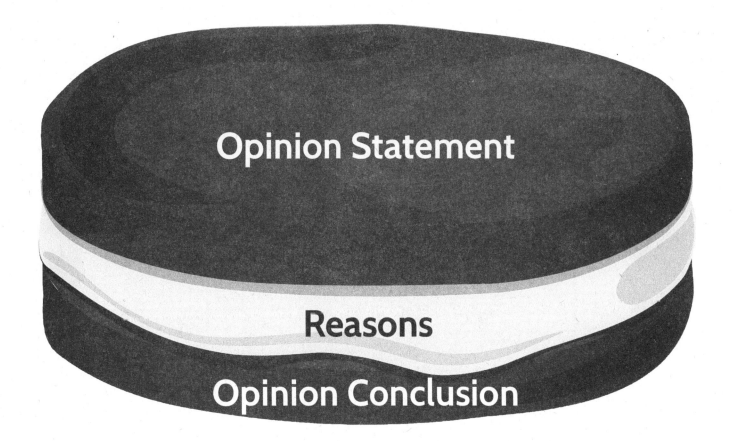

Name:

Handout 7A: Objects for Retelling

Directions: Use the following images to retell the story *Cendrillon.*

Name:

Handout 7B:
Cendrillon Opinion Paragraph

Directions: Cut on the dotted lines. Put the parts of the opinion paragraph in the correct sequence.

③ ------------------------------

That is why the ball scene is the best.

----

② Cendrillon has fun dancing with Paul.

I think the ball scene in *Cendrillon* is the best scene in the story.

----

①

Name:

Handout 8A: Focusing Question Task 1 Evidence Organizer

Directions: Complete the Evidence Organizer Chart using information from the Cinderella Traits Chart.

	Opinion Statement *Reasons* *Opinion Conclusion*	
O	Opinion Statement	
Re	Reasons	
O	Opinion Conclusion	That is why she is _____.

Handout 9A: Cinderella and Cendrillon Experience Cards

Directions: Cut apart the experience cards. Vote whether the experience is Cinderella's, Cendrillon's, or both.

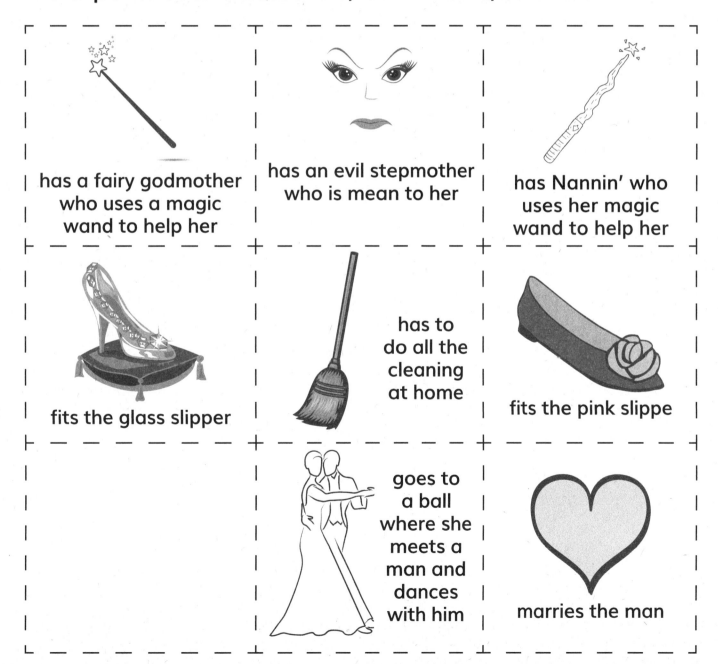

- has a fairy godmother who uses a magic wand to help her
- has an evil stepmother who is mean to her
- has Nannin' who uses her magic wand to help her
- fits the glass slipper
- has to do all the cleaning at home
- fits the pink slippe
- goes to a ball where she meets a man and dances with him
- marries the man

Name: _____

Handout 9B: Opinion Writing Checklist

Directions: Circle 🙂 Yes or 😐 Not Yet to answer each prompt.

Structure	Self	Peer	Teacher
I respond to all parts of the prompt.	🙂 😐 Yes Not Yet	🙂 😐 Yes Not Yet	🙂 😐 Yes Not Yet
I introduce the topic I am writing about.	🙂 😐 Yes Not Yet	🙂 😐 Yes Not Yet	🙂 😐 Yes Not Yet
I write an opinion statement.	🙂 😐 Yes Not Yet	🙂 😐 Yes Not Yet	🙂 😐 Yes Not Yet

Name:

I write one or more reasons to support my opinion statement.	☺ ☺ Yes Not Yet	☺ ☺ Yes Not Yet	☺ ☺ Yes Not Yet
I write a conclusion that reinforces my opinion.	☺ ☺ Yes Not Yet	☺ ☺ Yes Not Yet	☺ ☺ Yes Not Yet

Name: _____

Conventions	Self	Peer	Teacher
I use capital letters at the beginning of sentences and proper nouns.	☺ ☹ Yes Not Yet	☺ ☹ Yes Not Yet	☺ ☹ Yes Not Yet
I use end punctuation. **.?!**	☺ ☹ Yes Not Yet	☺ ☹ Yes Not Yet	☺ ☹ Yes Not Yet
I write complete sentences.	☺ ☹ Yes Not Yet	☺ ☹ Yes Not Yet	☺ ☹ Yes Not Yet
I use my best spelling. **ABC**	☺ ☹ Yes Not Yet	☺ ☹ Yes Not Yet	☺ ☹ Yes Not Yet
Total number of ☺			

Name:

Handout 10A: Objects for Retelling

Directions: Use the following images to retell the story The Rough-Face Girl.

Name:

Handout 11A: Fluency Homework

Directions: Choose one of the text options to read for homework. Read the entire passage. Have an adult or peer initial the unshaded boxes each day that you read the passage.

Option A

Adapted from *Bigfoot Cinderrrrrella* by Tony Johnston

Characters:
- Narrator
- Ella
- Beary Godfather

Narrator: How Rrrrrrela longed to go!
Sadly, she stared at the river.
She saw a fish jump.
She made a wish on the fish.

Ella: Me wish go fun-fest. Me wish dunk prince.

Beary Godfather: Heartfelt wish is true wish. And so, you go.

Narrator: Rrrrella spun around.
She was staring at the bear,
the very one she had given the fish.

Ella: Who you?

Beary Godfather: Me your beary godfather.

70 words

Johnston, Tony. *Bigfoot Cinderrrrrella*. Illustrated by James Warhola, 1998. Puffin Books, 2000.

Student Performance Checklist:	Day 1		Day 2		Day 3		Day 4		Day 5		Day 6	
	You	Listener*	You	Listener*	You	Listener*	You	Listener*	You	Listener*	You	Listener*
Read the passage three to five times.												
Read with appropriate phrasing and pausing.	▓	▓										
Read with appropriate expression.	▓	▓	▓	▓								
Read at a good pace, not too fast and not too slow.	▓	▓	▓	▓	▓	▓						
Read to be heard and understood.	▓	▓	▓	▓	▓	▓						

*Adult or peer

Name: _____

Option B

> Adapted from *Bigfoot Cinderrrrrella* by Tony Johnston
>
> Characters:
> - Narrator
> - Bigfoot Prince
> - Ella
>
> Narrator: The day grew late.
> Everyone had tried to win.
> Everyone had failed.
>
> Bigfoot Prince: Rrrrrrats! No brrrrride!
>
> Ella: Me dunk prince!
>
> Narrator: Grunting with all her might,
> she spun the log like a big twig.
> Then she gave it a twist and—flop!—
> the prince flopped into the river.
>
> 45 words
>
> Johnston, Tony. *Bigfoot Cinderrrrrella*. Illustrated by James Warhola, 1998. Puffin Books, 2000.

Student Performance Checklist:	Day 1		Day 2		Day 3		Day 4		Day 5		Day 6	
	You	Listener*	You	Listener*	You	Listener*	You	Listener*	You	Listener*	You	Listener*
Read the passage three to five times.												
Read with appropriate phrasing and pausing.												
Read with appropriate expression.												
Read at a good pace, not too fast and not too slow.												
Read to be heard and understood.												

*Adult or peer

Name:

Handout 11B: Commas in a Series

Directions: Combine these three simple sentences to create one sentence using the correct conjunction and comma placement.

- The Rough-Face Girl made a necklace.

- The Rough-Face Girl made a cap.

- The Rough-Face Girl made a dress.

Name:

Handout 13A: Story Map

Directions: Draw a picture or write to show the elements of the story.

Bigfoot Cinderrrrrella Story Map

Characters 	Setting 

Problem

Events

Resolution

Name: _____

Handout 13B: The Beary Godfather

Directions: Read the opinion statement. Then write a reason in the box underneath that supports the opinion statement.

I feel that the Beary Godfather is kind.

Reason

_____

_____

_____

That is why the Beary Godfather is kind.

Name: _____

Handout 14A: Word Cards

Directions: Cut apart the word cards and sort them into two categories: trees and not trees.

cedar	banana slug
Douglas firs	pine cones
wildflowers	deadfalls
coniferous	creature
Bigfoot	

Name:

Handout 15A: Focusing Question Task 2 Evidence Organizer

Directions: Complete the Evidence Organizer Chart using information from the Ella Traits Chart.

	Opinion Statement — Reasons — Opinion Conclusion	
O	Opinion Statement	
Re	Reasons	
O	Opinion Conclusion	That is why she is _____.

G1 > M4 > Handout 16A • WIT & WISDOM®

Name: _____

Handout 16A:
Cinderella and Ella Experience Cards

Directions: Cut apart the experience cards. Sort the cards according to whether the experiences are Cinderella's, Ella's, or both.

has to do all the cleaning at home	has an evil stepmother who is mean to her	has to fish for her family
has a fairy godmother who uses a magic wand to help her	goes to a party where she meets a prince	has a Beary Godfather who uses magic to help her
has combed hair and fancy clothes	marries the prince	has tangled fur and no fancy clothes

Page 1 of 2

Name:

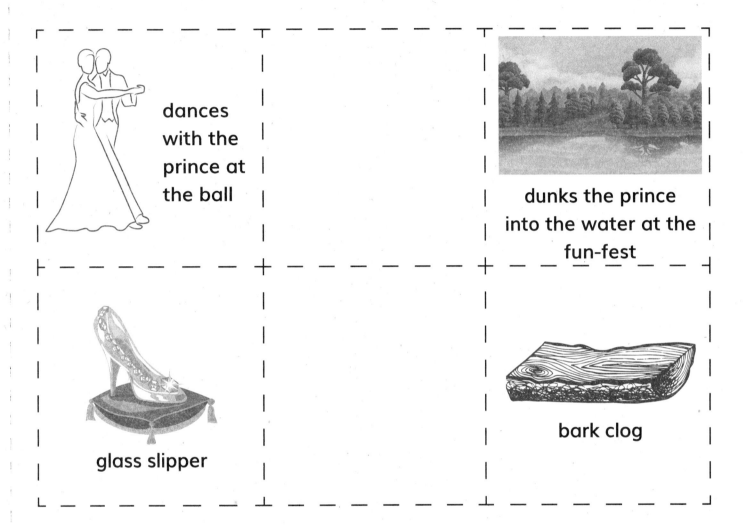

Name:

Handout 16B:
Opinion Writing Checklist

Directions: Circle 🙂 Yes or 😐 Not Yet to answer each prompt.

Structure	Self	Peer	Teacher
I respond to all parts of the prompt.	🙂 Yes 😐 Not Yet	🙂 Yes 😐 Not Yet	🙂 Yes 😐 Not Yet
I introduce the topic I am writing about.	🙂 Yes 😐 Not Yet	🙂 Yes 😐 Not Yet	🙂 Yes 😐 Not Yet
I write an opinion statement.	🙂 Yes 😐 Not Yet	🙂 Yes 😐 Not Yet	🙂 Yes 😐 Not Yet

Name:

I write one or more reasons to support my opinion statement.	☺ 😐 Yes Not Yet	☺ 😐 Yes Not Yet	☺ 😐 Yes Not Yet
I write a conclusion that reinforces my opinion.	☺ 😐 Yes Not Yet	☺ 😐 Yes Not Yet	☺ 😐 Yes Not Yet

Name: _____

Conventions	Self	Peer	Teacher
I use conjunctions. **and, or, but, because**	😊 😐 Yes Not Yet	😊 😐 Yes Not Yet	😊 😐 Yes Not Yet
I use capital letters at the beginning of sentences and proper nouns.	😊 😐 Yes Not Yet	😊 😐 Yes Not Yet	😊 😐 Yes Not Yet
I use end punctuation. **. ? !**	😊 😐 Yes Not Yet	😊 😐 Yes Not Yet	😊 😐 Yes Not Yet
I write complete sentences.	😊 😐 Yes Not Yet	😊 😐 Yes Not Yet	😊 😐 Yes Not Yet
I use my best spelling. **ABC**	😊 😐 Yes Not Yet	😊 😐 Yes Not Yet	😊 😐 Yes Not Yet
Total number of 😊			

Name:

Handout 17A: Fluency Homework

Directions: Read the entire passage. Have an adult or peer initial the unshaded boxes each day that you read the passage.

Adapted from *Adelita* by Tomie dePaola

Characters:
- Javier
- Doña Micaela
- Adelita
- Narrator

Javier: Yes, ladies, I remember you,
   but it's another that I'm looking for.

Doña Micaela: There's no one else here.

Adelita: Yes, there is. Are you looking for me, Señor?

Narrator: There was Adelita,
   standing at the top of the stairs
   in her mother's dress and rebozo.

Javier: My Cenicienta.

Narrator: Javier asked Adelita to marry him.

Javier and Adelita: We shall live happily ever after.

Everyone: And they did.

59 words

dePaola, Tomie. *Adelita*. 2002. Puffin Books, 2004.

Student Performance Checklist:	Day 1 You	Day 1 Listener*	Day 2 You	Day 2 Listener*	Day 3 You	Day 3 Listener*	Day 4 You	Day 4 Listener*	Day 5 You	Day 5 Listener*
Read the passage three to five times.										
Read with appropriate phrasing and pausing.	▓	▓								
Read with appropriate expression.	▓	▓	▓	▓						
Read at a good pace, not too fast and not too slow.	▓	▓	▓	▓	▓	▓				
Read to be heard and understood.	▓	▓	▓	▓	▓	▓				

*Adult or peer

Name: _____

Handout 17B: Word Cards

Directions: Cut apart the word cards.

meager	despair
magnificent	fiesta
stunning	honored

Name:

Handout 18A: Story Map

Directions: Draw a picture or write to show the elements of the story.

Adelita Story Map

Characters	Setting

Problem

Events

Resolution

Name:

Handout 18B: Pronoun Practice

Directions: Circle the correct pronoun to replace the underlined noun or nouns in the sentence.

- My sister went to school yesterday. (*he, she*)

- Karen and I had fun at the park. (*we, they*)

- Lisa's dog was lost. (*her, his*)

- Miguel's dad came to school to eat lunch. (*her, his*)

Name: _____

Handout 19A: *Adelita* Action Cards

Directions: Cut out the action cards. Use the actions on the cards to Link Up with other students with similar actions.

Name:

Handout 19B: Pronoun Practice

Directions: Circle the correct indefinite pronoun to complete the sentence.

- We could not go _____ because it was raining.

    (*everywhere, anywhere*)

- _____ was going to school because it was a snow day.

    (*anybody, nobody*)

- I couldn't find my backpack _____.

    (*anywhere, nowhere*)

- My sister looked _____ for her pencil.

    (*nowhere, everywhere*)

Name:

Handout 21A: Venn Diagram

Directions: Sort the experience cards into the correct spot on the Venn diagram.

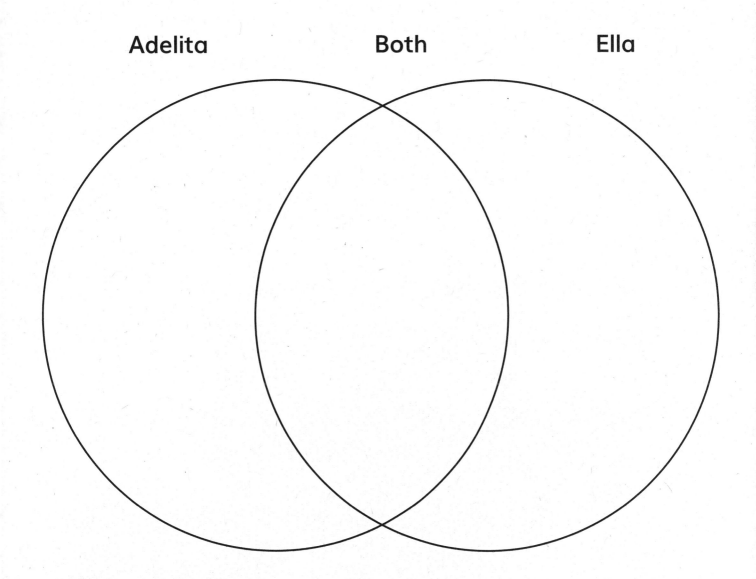

Handout 21B:
Ella and Adelita Experience Cards

Directions: Cut apart the experience cards. Sort the cards into a Venn diagram to identify whether the experiences are Ella's, Adelita's, or both.

Name: _____

Handout 21C: The Rebozo

Directions: Follow along as your teacher reads a paragraph that responds to the question "Which proof of identity do you think is the best, the bark clog or the rebozo?" Write an introduction to the opinion paragraph on the lines below.

_____

_____

_____

In my opinion, the rebozo is the best proof of identity. Javier saw the rebozo hanging in the window. He knew the girl was in the house. That is why the rebozo is the best proof of identity.

Name:

Handout 22A: Fluency Homework

Directions: Choose one of the text options to read for homework. Read the entire passage. Have an adult or peer initial the unshaded boxes each day that you read the passage.

Option A

Adapted from *The Korean Cinderella* by Shirley Climo

Characters:
- Narrator
- Omoni
- Pear Blossom

Narrator: Omoni found fault as soon as she stepped into the kitchen.

Omoni: Too cold.
   The fire's gone out.
   Fetch wood, Pear Blossom.
   Be quick!

Narrator: Pear Blossom gathered sticks and fed the stove
   until the lid on the kettle danced from steam.

Omoni: Too hot!
   The noodles are scorching.
   Get water, Pear Blossom.
   Be quick!

Narrator: Both Omoni and Peony were jealous of Pear Blossom,
   and the harder she worked the happier they were.
   Each day, Pear Blossom was up before the sun.
   She cooked and cleaned until midnight,
   with only the crickets for company.

89 words

Climo, Shirley. *The Korean Cinderella*. Illustrated by Ruth Heller, HarperCollins Children's Books, 1993.

Student Performance Checklist:	Day 1		Day 2		Day 3		Day 4		Day 5		Day 6	
	You	Listener*	You	Listener*	You	Listener*	You	Listener*	You	Listener*	You	Listener*
Read the passage three to five times.												
Read with appropriate phrasing and pausing.	▓	▓										
Read with appropriate expression.	▓	▓	▓	▓								
Read at a good pace, not too fast and not too slow.	▓	▓	▓	▓	▓	▓						
Read to be heard and understood.	▓	▓	▓	▓	▓	▓						

*Adult or peer

Name:

Option B

Adapted from *The Korean Cinderella* by Shirley Climo

Characters:
- Narrator
- Omoni
- Pear Blossom

Narrator: Omoni found fault as soon as she stepped into the kitchen.

Omoni: Too cold.
    The fire's gone out.
    Fetch wood, Pear Blossom.
    Be quick!

Narrator: Pear Blossom gathered sticks and fed the stove
    until the lid on the kettle danced from steam.

Omoni: Too hot!
    The noodles are scorching.
    Get water, Pear Blossom.
    Be quick!

Narrator: Both Omoni and Peony were jealous of Pear Blossom,
    and the harder she worked the happier they were.
    Each day, Pear Blossom was up before the sun.
    She cooked and cleaned until midnight, with only the crickets for company.

Narrator: But nothing could hide Pear Blossom's beauty.
    At night Omoni lay sleepless,
    searching for an excuse to get rid of her stepdaughter.

112 words

Climo, Shirley. *The Korean Cinderella*. Illustrated by Ruth Heller, HarperCollins Children's Books, 1993.

G1 > M4 > Handout 22A • WIT & WISDOM®

Student Performance Checklist:	Day 1		Day 2		Day 3		Day 4		Day 5		Day 6	
	You	Listener*	You	Listener*	You	Listener*	You	Listener*	You	Listener*	You	Listener*
Read the passage three to five times.												
Read with appropriate phrasing and pausing.	▓	▓										
Read with appropriate expression.	▓	▓	▓	▓								
Read at a good pace, not too fast and not too slow.	▓	▓	▓	▓	▓	▓						
Read to be heard and understood.	▓	▓	▓	▓	▓	▓						

*Adult or peer

Name:

Handout 23A: Story Map

Directions: Draw a picture or write to show the elements of the story.

The Korean Cinderella Story Map

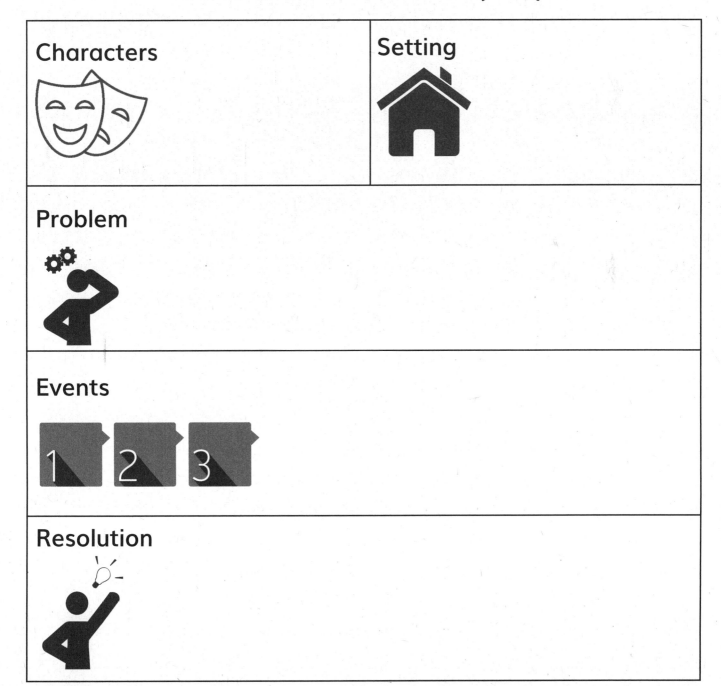

Name:

Handout 24A:
Pear Blossom Action Cards

Directions: Cut out the action cards. Use actions to Link Up with other students with similar actions.

Pear Blossom cooks and cleans all day.

Pear Blossom tells the truth about the frog that helps her.

Pear Blossom packs food and sews clothes for her stepmother and stepsister.

Pear Blossom tells the truth about the sparrows who help her.

Name: _____

Handout 24B: Focusing Question Task 3 Evidence Organizer

Directions: Complete the Evidence Organizer Chart using information from the Adelita or Pear Blossom Traits Chart.

Circle the character's name you will be writing about:

Adelita   Pear Blossom

I	Introduction	
O	Opinion Statement	
Re	Reasons	
O	Opinion Conclusion	

Name:

Handout 25A:
Illustration Scavenger Hunt

Directions: Find the illustrations below in the text *The Korean Cinderella* and put a sticky note on the page(s) on which they appear.

Name:

Handout 25B: Content Word Sort

Directions: Write the category titles at the top of the chart. Cut out the word cards from the bottom. Sort the words into the correct categories on the chart.

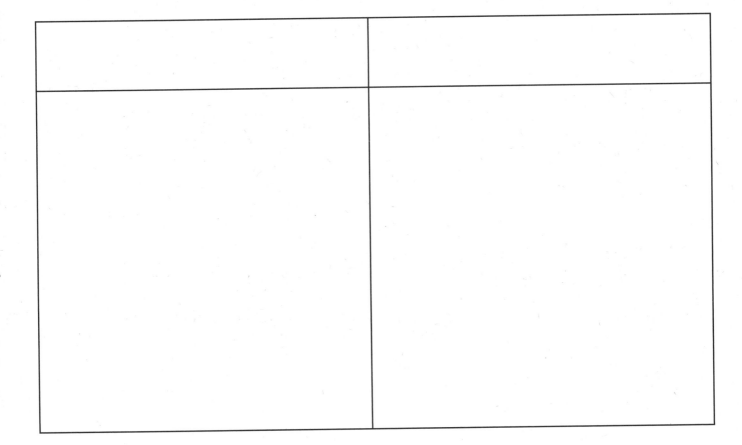

frog	cabbage
rice	sparrow
barley sugar	black ox
turnips	honey candy

Name: _____

Handout 26A:
Opinion Writing Checklist

Directions: Circle 🙂 Yes or 😐 Not Yet to answer each prompt.

Structure	Self	Peer	Teacher
I respond to all parts of the prompt.	🙂 Yes 😐 Not Yet	🙂 Yes 😐 Not Yet	🙂 Yes 😐 Not Yet
I introduce the topic I am writing about.	🙂 Yes 😐 Not Yet	🙂 Yes 😐 Not Yet	🙂 Yes 😐 Not Yet
I write an opinion statement.	🙂 Yes 😐 Not Yet	🙂 Yes 😐 Not Yet	🙂 Yes 😐 Not Yet
I write one or more reasons to support my opinion statement.	🙂 Yes 😐 Not Yet	🙂 Yes 😐 Not Yet	🙂 Yes 😐 Not Yet

	Self	Peer	Teacher
I write a conclusion that reinforces my opinion.	Yes Not Yet	Yes Not Yet	Yes Not Yet
Conventions	**Self**	**Peer**	**Teacher**
I use conjunctions. **and, or, but, because**	Yes Not Yet	Yes Not Yet	Yes Not Yet
I use capital letters at the beginning of sentences and proper nouns.	Yes Not Yet	Yes Not Yet	Yes Not Yet
I use end punctuation. **.?!**	Yes Not Yet	Yes Not Yet	Yes Not Yet
I write complete sentences.	Yes Not Yet	Yes Not Yet	Yes Not Yet
I use my best spelling. **ABC**	Yes Not Yet	Yes Not Yet	Yes Not Yet
Total number of 🙂			

Name: _____

Handout 26B: Sentence Frames

Directions: Circle the correct verb to complete the sentences.

- The sun is _____ today! It's almost a hundred degrees outside.

  (*scorching, scorched*)

- "I won!" the boy _____ after hitting the final shot of the game.

  (*exclaiming, exclaimed*)

- The bird is _____ on the fence post.

  (*perching, perched*)

- The swing _____ in the wind.

  (*swaying, swayed*)

- The squirrel is _____ nuts and storing them for winter.

  (*gathering, gathered*)

Name: _____

Handout 27A: "900 Cinderellas"

Directions: Listen carefully as your teacher reads an excerpt from the article "900 Cinderellas." Signal when you hear information that connects to, or is the same as, other Cinderella stories you have read.

Excerpt from "900 Cinderellas"

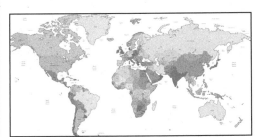

If someone asked you to name a fairy tale everyone knows, chances are you might say *Cinderella*. But did you know that the story of Cinderella is found all over the world in many different cultures? In China, she is known as Yeh-Shen. In Appalachia, she is called Ashpet. Some Native Americans know her as Little Burnt Face.

No matter what she is called, Cinderella is always beautiful and good. Sadly, other members of her family are jealous of her goodness and beauty. They are cruel to her. She is made to wear rags and do the worst chores in the household. But then a magical person comes to help her. Dressed in beautiful clothes, Cinderella meets a prince or a king who wants to marry her, but she is forced to run away from him and wear her rags again. In the end, he finds Cinderella, after she proves her identity through a special test (remember the glass slipper?). Then they marry and live happily ever after. Around the world, there are more than 900 different versions of this story, but they all follow this same basic plot.

Excerpt from Lusted, Marcia Amidon and Judith C. Greenfield. "900 Cinderellas." *Appleseeds*, vol. 11, no. 5, Feb. 2009, pp. 9–11. *Cricket Media*, Carus Publishing Company.

Name:

Handout 28A: Word Cards

Directions: Cut apart the word cards.

sugarcane	honey
figs	apricots
rice	mangoes
melons	beef stew
cookies	custards
slippers	anklets
sandals	shoes
robe	sarong
cloak	kimono

Name:

Handout 30A: Textile Patterns

Directions: Use the patterns below to find similar designs in *Glass Slipper, Gold Sandal*.

Name:

Handout 30B: End-of-Module Task Evidence Organizer Chart

Directions: Use the Evidence Organizer Chart to plan your opinion paragraph.

		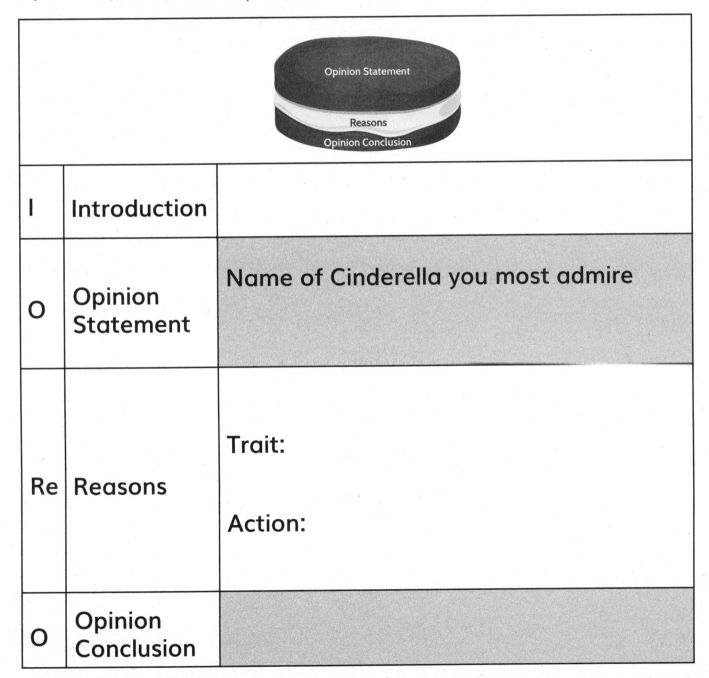
I	Introduction	
O	Opinion Statement	Name of Cinderella you most admire
Re	Reasons	Trait: Action:
O	Opinion Conclusion	

Name:

Handout 32A:
Opinion Writing Checklist

Directions: Circle 🙂 Yes or ☹ Not Yet to answer each prompt.

Structure	Self	Peer	Teacher
I respond to all parts of the prompt.	Yes Not Yet	Yes Not Yet	Yes Not Yet
I introduce the topic I am writing about.	Yes Not Yet	Yes Not Yet	Yes Not Yet
I write an opinion statement.	Yes Not Yet	Yes Not Yet	Yes Not Yet
I write one or more reasons to support my opinion statement.	Yes Not Yet	Yes Not Yet	Yes Not Yet

	Self	Peer	Teacher
I write a conclusion that reinforces my opinion. *(Opinion Statement / Reasons / Opinion Conclusion)*	☺ Yes ☹ Not Yet	☺ Yes ☹ Not Yet	☺ Yes ☹ Not Yet
Conventions	Self	Peer	Teacher
I use conjunctions. **and, or, but, because**	☺ Yes ☹ Not Yet	☺ Yes ☹ Not Yet	☺ Yes ☹ Not Yet
I use capital letters at the beginning of sentences and proper nouns.	☺ Yes ☹ Not Yet	☺ Yes ☹ Not Yet	☺ Yes ☹ Not Yet
I use end punctuation. **. ? !**	☺ Yes ☹ Not Yet	☺ Yes ☹ Not Yet	☺ Yes ☹ Not Yet
I write complete sentences.	☺ Yes ☹ Not Yet	☺ Yes ☹ Not Yet	☺ Yes ☹ Not Yet
I use my best spelling. **ABC**	☺ Yes ☹ Not Yet	☺ Yes ☹ Not Yet	☺ Yes ☹ Not Yet
Total number of ☺			

Name: _____

Handout 34A:
Socratic Seminar Self-Reflection

Directions: Use one of the letters below to describe how often you performed each action during the Socratic Seminar.

A = I always did that.

S = I sometimes did that.

N = I'll do that next time.

Expectation	Evaluation (A, S, N)
I noticed the whole message.	
I linked what I said to what others said.	
I looked at the speaker.	
I spoke only when no one else was speaking.	
I used kind words.	

Name:

Volume of Reading Reflection Questions

Cinderella Stories, Grade 1, Module 4

Student Name:

Text:

Author:

Topic:

Genre/type of book:

Share what you know by answering the questions. Draw, write, or tell your teacher your answers.

Informational Texts

1. **Wonder:** What do you notice when you look at the title and illustrations on the cover of this book? What are the clues about places discussed in this book?

2. **Organize:** What are the main ideas of this book? How do the illustrations help with showing more details?

3. **Reveal:** How does the author use capital letters in this text? Find one example of a capitalized place, a capitalized character name, and a capitalized beginning of a sentence or title.

4. **Distill:** What is the most important idea that you learned by reading this text? Draw a picture showing this idea and explain your drawing on the paper to the class or to your teacher.

5. **Know:** What new information do you now know after reading this book? Explain how this information compares to a different book about the same topic. Is it the same information, or is it different information? Explain.

6. **Vocabulary:** In the text, find a color word, a clothing word, or a place word. Try to find four new words to add to your word collection. For example, if the word is *Mexico*, come up with four other places to make a place collection. If the word is *dress*, come up with four other clothing words to make a clothing collection.

Literary Texts

1. **Wonder:** Look at the illustrations on the cover. What do you notice and wonder about the setting of the story?

2. **Organize:** What happened in this story? Tell how the author and illustrator told the story through both pictures and words. Be sure to discuss the characters, settings, and events.

3. **Reveal:** Find a place in the story where there is dialogue. Tell who is telling the story as each character speaks. If you are able, take turns reading the dialogue with another person, reading the different parts in different voices.

4. **Distill:** Did this story teach you a life lesson? What lesson did it teach?

5. **Know:** How does this text add to your knowledge about Cinderella stories or fairy tales in general? How does this story compare to other stories you have read?

6. **Vocabulary:** In this set of lessons, we have talked about the word *admire*. In your opinion, which character do you most admire in this story? Support your choice with reasons from the text.

WIT & WISDOM FAMILY TIP SHEET

WHAT IS MY GRADE 1 STUDENT LEARNING IN MODULE 4?

Wit & Wisdom is our English curriculum. It builds knowledge of key topics in history, science, and literature through the study of excellent texts. By reading and responding to stories and nonfiction texts, we will build knowledge of the following topics:

Module 1: A World of Books

Module 2: Creature Features

Module 3: Powerful Forces

Module 4: Cinderella Stories

In Module 4, *Cinderella Stories*, students discover that while there are thousands of versions of the Cinderella story, the stories are united by common elements and themes. Changes to the setting do not disrupt the magic of these tales or their ability to impart the importance of kindness, forgiveness, and belief in good triumphing over evil. We will ask the question: *Why do people around the world admire Cinderella?*

OUR CLASS WILL READ THESE BOOKS:

Picture Books (Literary)

- *Cinderella,* Marcia Brown
- *Cendrillon: A Caribbean Cinderella,* Robert D. San Souci; Illustrations, Brian Pinkney
- *The Rough-Face Girl,* Rafe Martin; Illustrations, David Shannon
- *Bigfoot Cinderrrrrella,* Tony Johnston; Illustrations, James Warhola
- *The Korean Cinderella,* Shirley Climo; Illustrations, Ruth Heller
- *Adelita,* Tomie dePaola
- *Glass Slipper, Gold Sandal: A Worldwide Cinderella,* Paul Fleischman; Illustrations, Julie Paschkis

OUR CLASS WILL WATCH THESE VIDEOS:

- "Kudhinda Screen Printing"
- "The Process of Making Batik—Artisans at work"
- "Wycinanka/Paper Cutout"

OUR CLASS WILL READ THESE ARTICLES:

- "900 Cinderellas," Marcia Amidon Lusted and Judith C. Greenfield

OUR CLASS WILL EXAMINE THESE PAINTINGS:

- *First Steps,* Jean-Francois Millet
- *First Steps, after Millet,* Vincent van Gogh
- *First Steps,* Pablo Picasso

OUR CLASS WILL VISIT THESE WEBSITES:
- "Around the World," TIME for Kids
- "Talking Textiles," The Children's University of Manchester

OUR CLASS WILL ASK THESE QUESTIONS:
- Why do people admire Perrault's Cinderella?
- Why do people admire Rough-Face Girl and Ella?
- Why do people admire Adelita and Pear Blossom?

QUESTIONS TO ASK AT HOME:

As you read with your Grade 1 student, ask the following:

- How does this text build your knowledge of Cinderella stories? Share what you know about Cinderella stories.

BOOKS TO READ AT HOME:
- Mufaro's Beautiful Daughters, John Steptoe
- Sootface: An Ojibwa Cinderella Story, Robert D. San Souci
- Cinderella/Centicienta*, Francesc Boada
- Vincent van Gogh (Getting to Know the Artist), Mike Venezia
- Pablo Picasso (Getting to Know the Artist), Mike Venezia
- Cinderella Penguin, Janet Perlman
- The Irish Cinderlad, Shirley Climo
- A Cinderella from China, Ai-Ling Louie
- Lon Po Po: A Red-Riding Hood Story from China, Ed Young
- The Golden Sandal: A Middle Eastern Cinderella Story, Rebecca Hickox
- Spotlight on South Korea, Bobbie Kalman
- This is Ireland, Miroslav Sasek
- Vincent's Colors, Vincent van Gogh, The Metropolitan Museum of Art

*This text is written in both English and Spanish.

IDEAS FOR TALKING ABOUT CINDERELLA STORIES:
- Visit a library together. Ask the librarian to recommend another book about Cinderella, or select one of the titles from the list above. As you read the text with your child, ask the following:
  - What traits do you admire about the Cinderella character?
  - What traits do you not admire about some of the other characters in the story?
  - What elements of Cinderella stories do you recognize? Follow up with the following: What are the good and evil characters, magical element, and proof of identity in this story?
  - What are some similarities and differences between the Cinderella character in this story and that character in another Cinderella story that we read?
  - Who was telling the story in this part we just read? How do you know?

CREDITS

Great Minds® has made every effort to obtain permission for the reprinting of all copyrighted material. If any owner of copyrighted material is not acknowledged herein, please contact Great Minds® for proper acknowledgment in all future editions and reprints of this module.

- All material from the *Common Core State Standards for English Language Arts & Literacy in History/Social Studies, Science, and Technical Subjects* © Copyright 2010 National Governors Association Center for Best Practices and Council of Chief State School Officers. All rights reserved.

- All images are used under license from Shutterstock.com unless otherwise noted.

- Handout 27A and Assessment 33A: "900 Cinderellas" by Marcia Amidon Lusted and Judith C. Greenfield from *Tell Me a Story*, Appleseeds February 2009. Text copyright © 2009 by Carus Publishing Company. Reprinted by permission of Cricket Media. All Cricket Media material is copyrighted by Carus Publishing d/b/a Cricket Media, and/or various authors and illustrators. Any commercial use or distribution of material without permission is strictly prohibited. Please visit **http://www.cricketmedia.com/info/licensing2** for licensing and **http://www.cricketmedia.com** for subscriptions.

- For updated credit information, please visit **http://witeng.link/credits**.

ACKNOWLEDGMENTS

Great Minds® Staff

The following writers, editors, reviewers, and support staff contributed to the development of this curriculum.

Karen Aleo, Elizabeth Bailey, Ashley Bessicks, Sarah Brenner, Ann Brigham, Catherine Cafferty, Sheila Byrd-Carmichael, Lauren Chapalee, Emily Climer, Rebecca Cohen, Elaine Collins, Julia Dantchev, Beverly Davis, Shana Dinner de Vaca, Kristy Ellis, Moira Clarkin Evans, Marty Gephart, Mamie Goodson, Nora Graham, Lindsay Griffith, Lorraine Griffith, Christina Gonzalez, Emily Gula, Brenna Haffner, Joanna Hawkins, Elizabeth Haydel, Sarah Henchey, Trish Huerster, Ashley Hymel, Carol Jago, Mica Jochim, Jennifer Johnson, Mason Judy, Sara Judy, Lior Klirs, Shelly Knupp, Liana Krissoff, Sarah Kushner, Suzanne Lauchaire, Diana Leddy, David Liben, Farren Liben, Brittany Lowe, Whitney Lyle, Stephanie Kane-Mainier, Liz Manolis, Jennifer Marin, Audrey Mastroleo, Maya Marquez, Susannah Maynard, Cathy McGath, Emily McKean, Andrea Minich, Rebecca Moore, Lynne Munson, Carol Paiva, Michelle Palmieri, Tricia Parker, Marya Myers Parr, Meredith Phillips, Eden Plantz, Shilpa Raman, Rachel Rooney, Jennifer Ruppel, Julie Sawyer-Wood, Nicole Shivers, Danielle Shylit, Rachel Stack, Amelia Swabb, Vicki Taylor, Melissa Thomson, Lindsay Tomlinson, Tsianina Tovar, Sarah Turnage, Melissa Vail, Keenan Walsh, Michelle Warner, Julia Wasson, Katie Waters, Sarah Webb, Lynn Welch, Yvonne Guerrero Welch, Amy Wierzbicki, Margaret Wilson, Sarah Woodard, Lynn Woods, and Rachel Zindler

Colleagues and Contributors

We are grateful for the many educators, writers, and subject-matter experts who made this program possible.

David Abel, Robin Agurkis, Sarah Ambrose, Rebeca Barroso, Julianne Barto, Amy Benjamin, Andrew Biemiller, Charlotte Boucher, Adam Cardais, Eric Carey, Jessica Carloni, Dawn Cavalieri, Janine Cody, Tequila Cornelious, David Cummings, Matt Davis, Thomas Easterling, Jeanette Edelstein, Sandra Engleman, Charles Fischer, Kath Gibbs, Natalie Goldstein, Laurie Gonsoulin, Dennis Hamel, Kristen Hayes, Steve Hettleman, Cara Hoppe, Libby Howard, Gail Kearns, Lisa King, Sarah Kopec, Andrew Krepp, Shannon Last, Ted MacInnis, Christina Martire, Alisha McCarthy, Cindy Medici, Brian Methe, Ivonne Mercado, Patricia Mickelberry, Jane Miller, Cathy Newton, Turi Nilsson, Julie Norris, Tara O'Hare, Galemarie Ola, Tamara Otto, Christine Palmtag, Dave Powers, Jeff Robinson, Karen Rollhauser, Tonya Romayne, Emmet Rosenfeld, Mike Russoniello, Deborah Samley, Casey Schultz, Renee Simpson, Rebecca Sklepovich, Kim Taylor, Tracy Vigliotti, Charmaine Whitman, Glenda Wisenburn-Burke, and Howard Yaffe

Early Adopters

The following early adopters provided invaluable insight and guidance for Wit & Wisdom:

- Bourbonnais School District 53 • Bourbonnais, IL
- Coney Island Prep Middle School • Brooklyn, NY
- Gate City Charter School for the Arts • Merrimack, NH
- Hebrew Academy for Special Children • Brooklyn, NY
- Paris Independent Schools • Paris, KY
- Saydel Community School District • Saydel, IA
- Strive Collegiate Academy • Nashville, TN
- Valiente College Preparatory Charter School • South Gate, CA
- Voyageur Academy • Detroit, MI

Design Direction provided by Alton Creative, Inc.

Project management support, production design and copyediting services provided by ScribeConcepts.com

Copyediting services provided by Fine Lines Editing

Product management support provided by Sandhill Consulting